CAT COLORING BOOKS

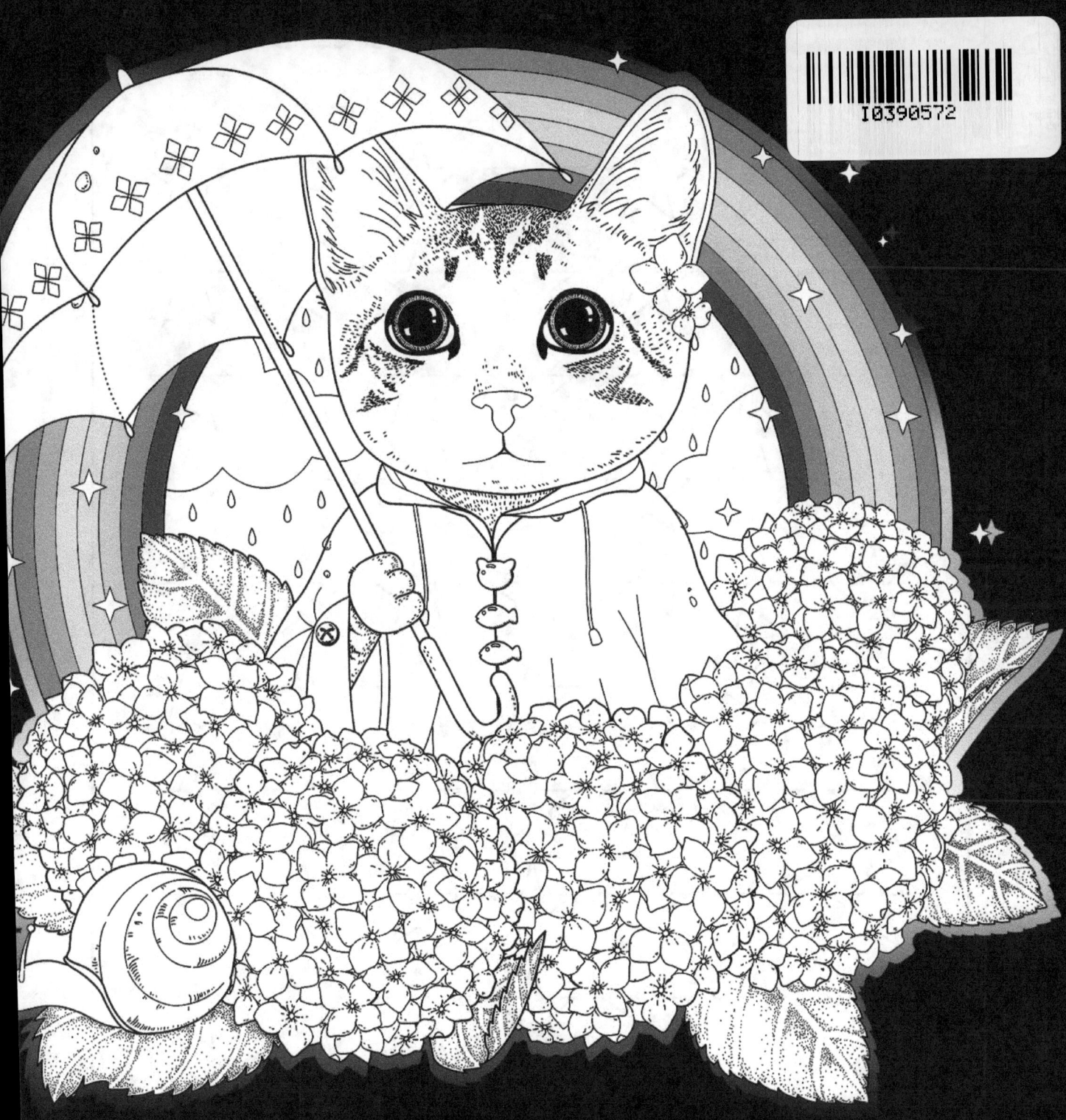

Animal Designs and Stress Relieving Patterns for Relaxation

TEST YOUR COLOR

TEST YOUR COLOR

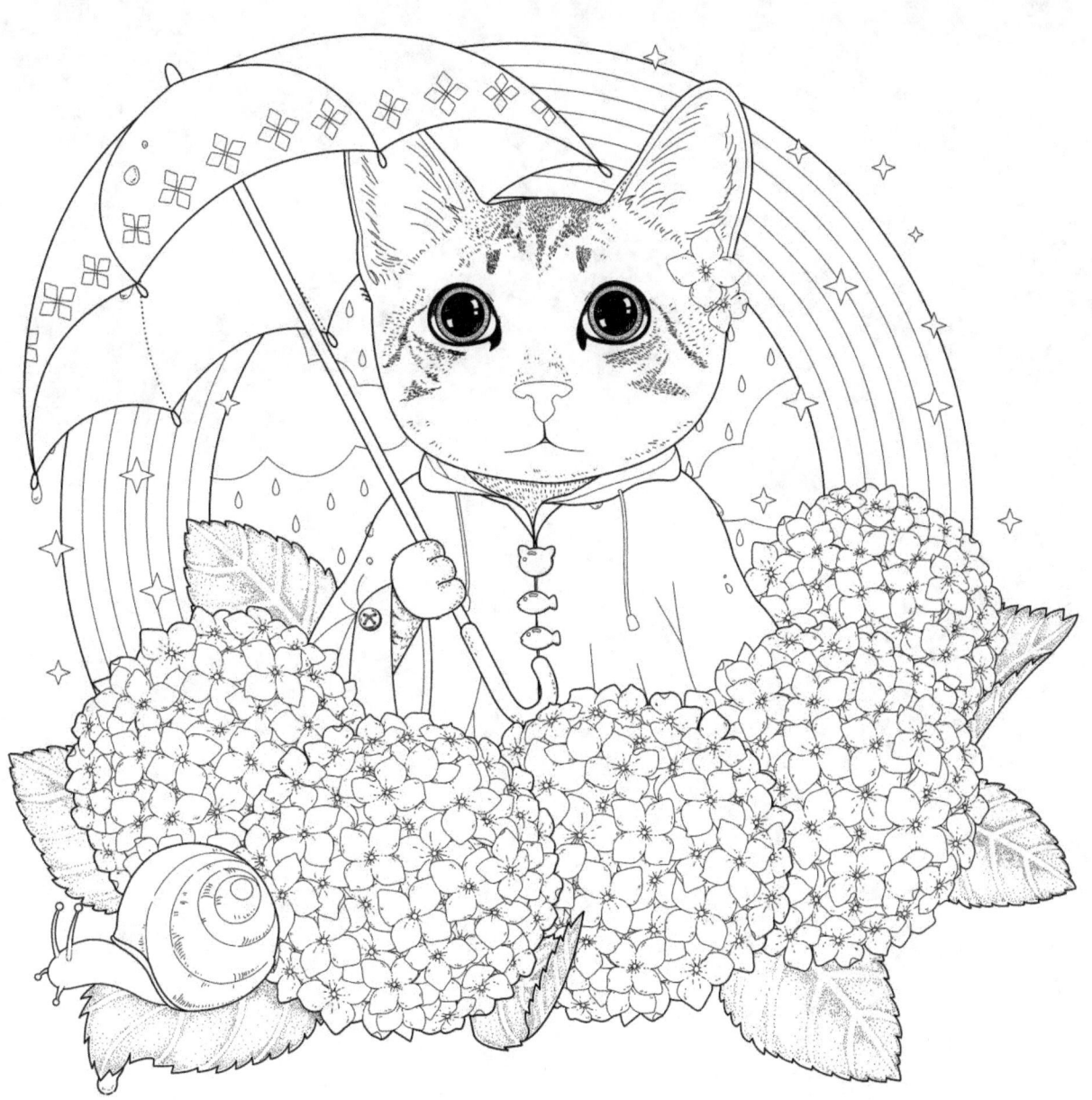

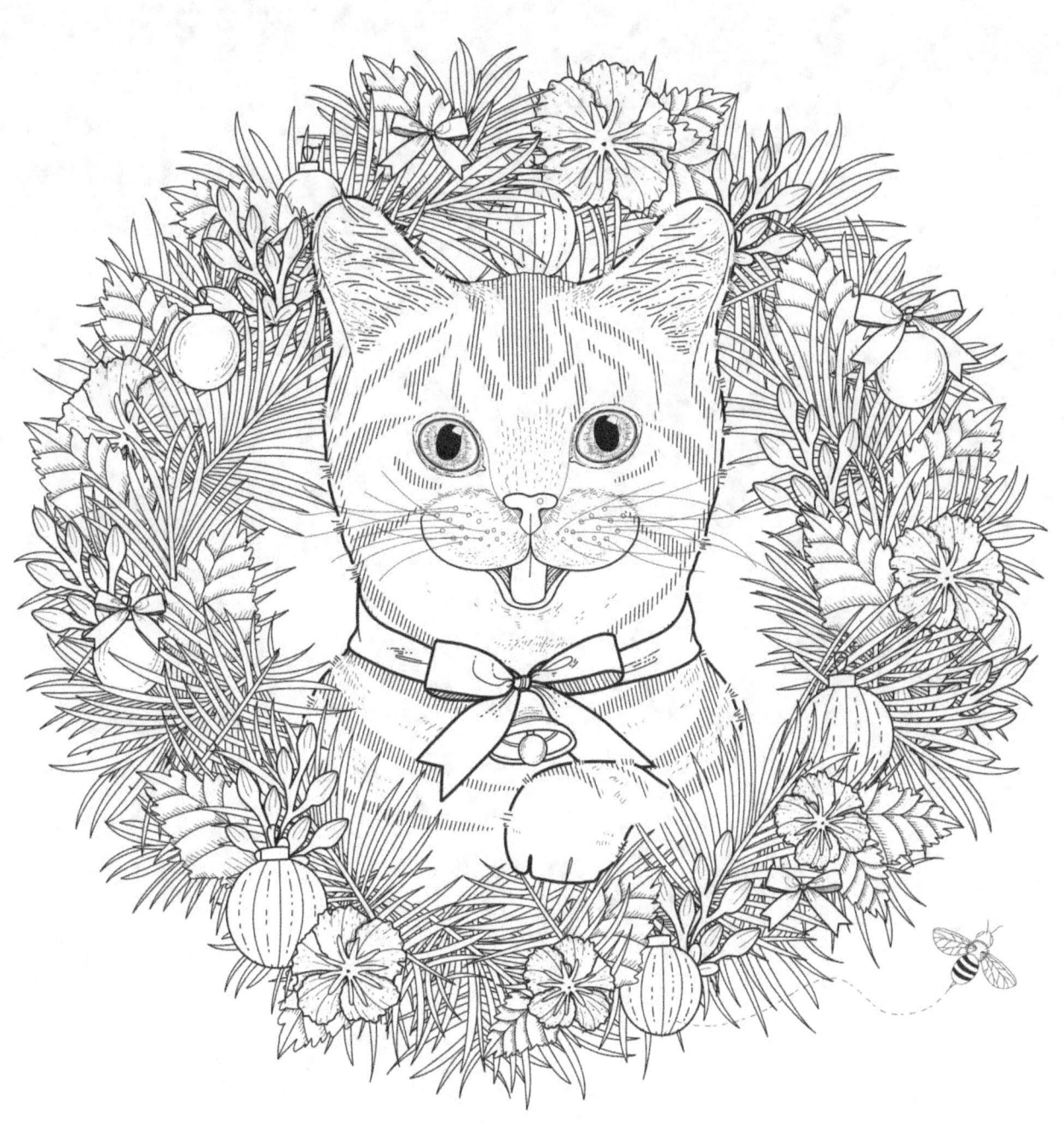

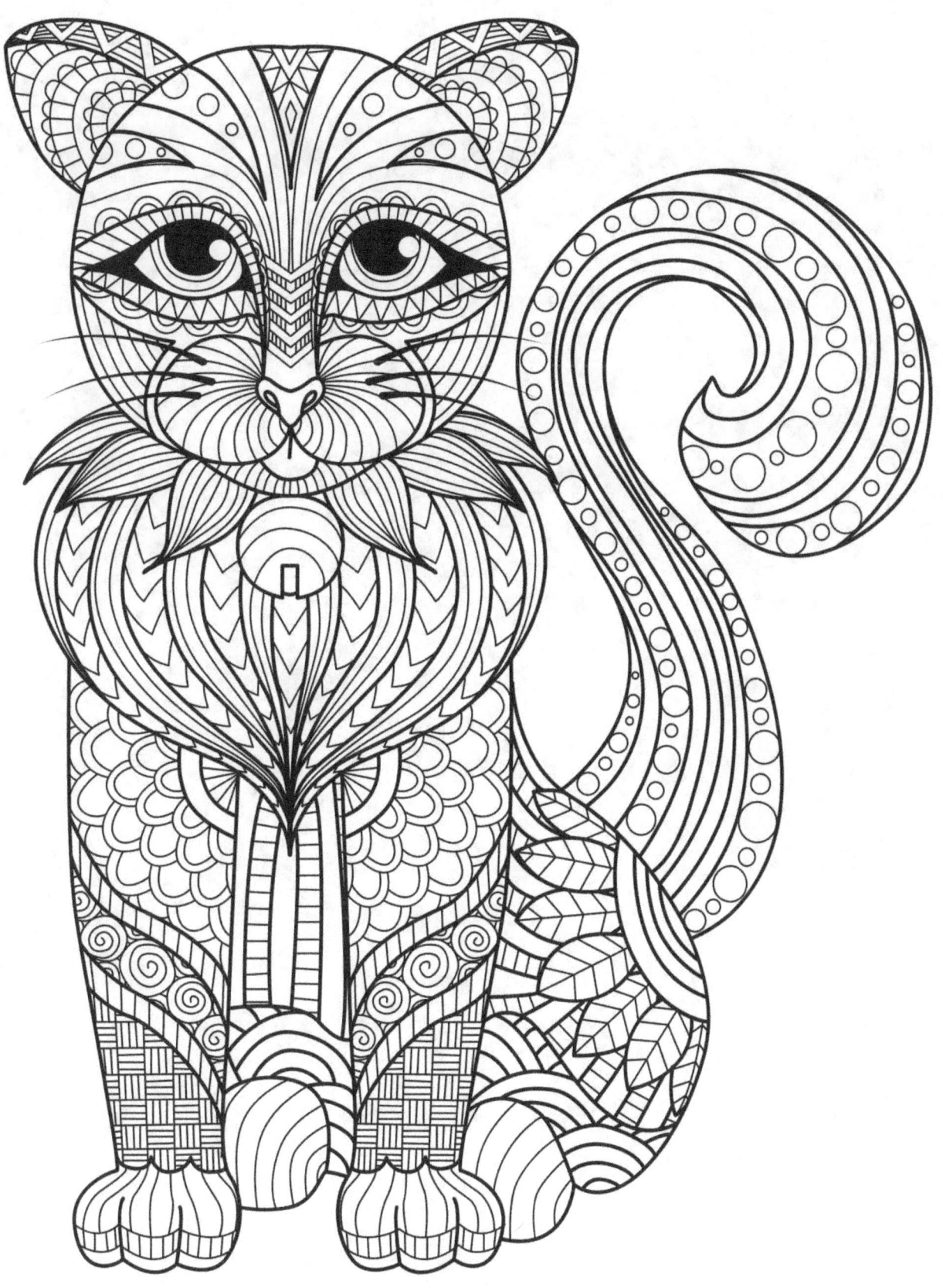

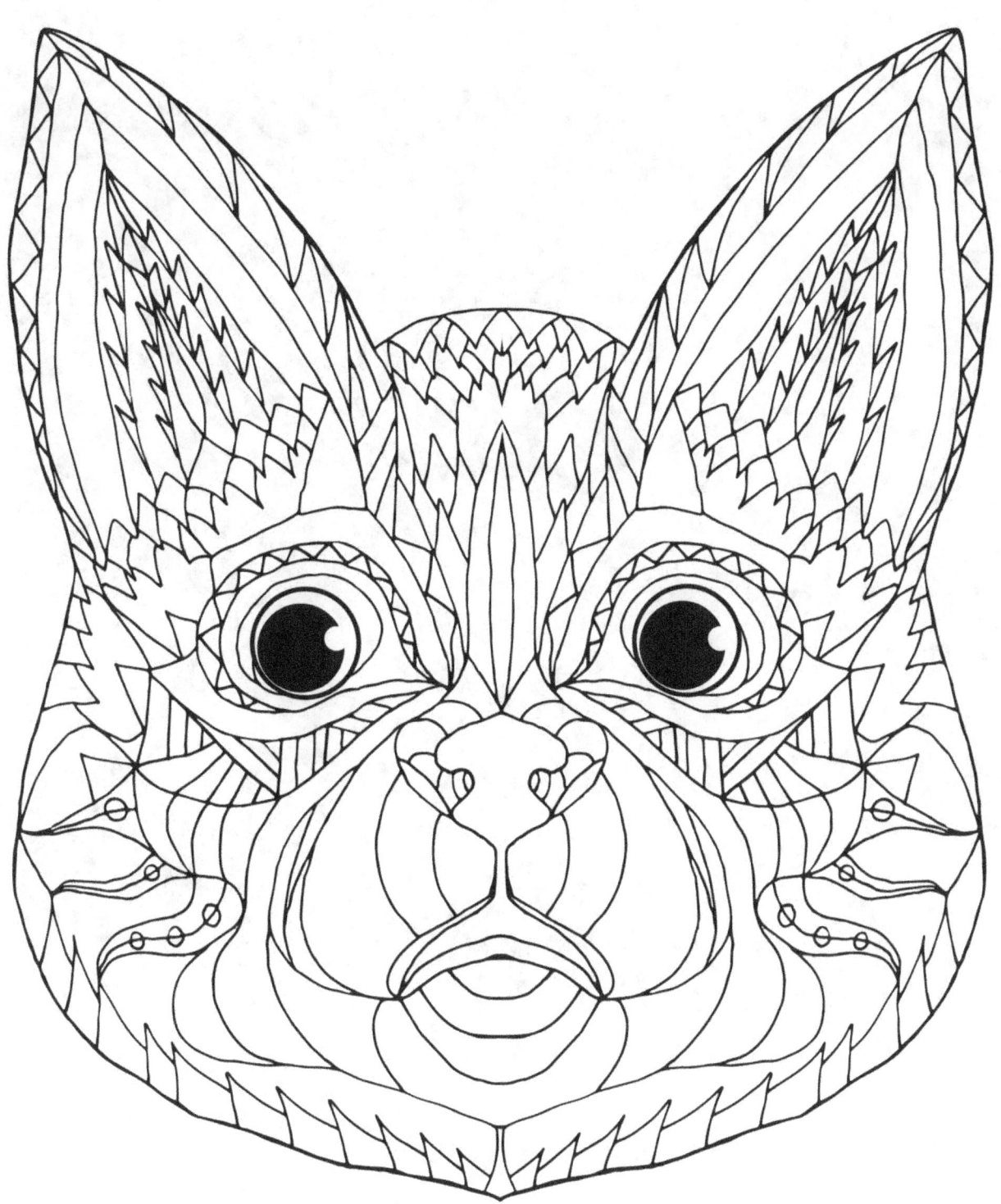

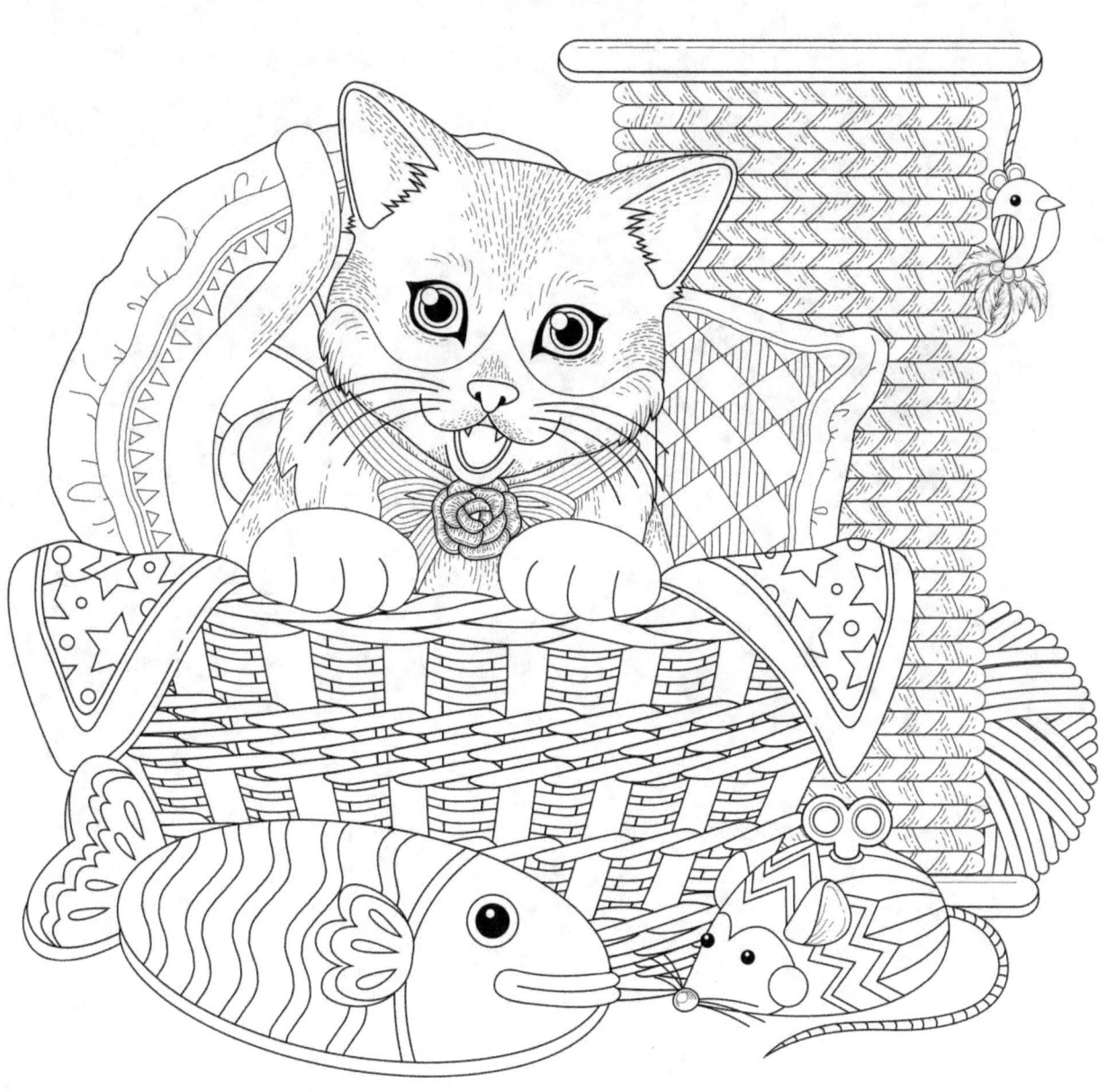

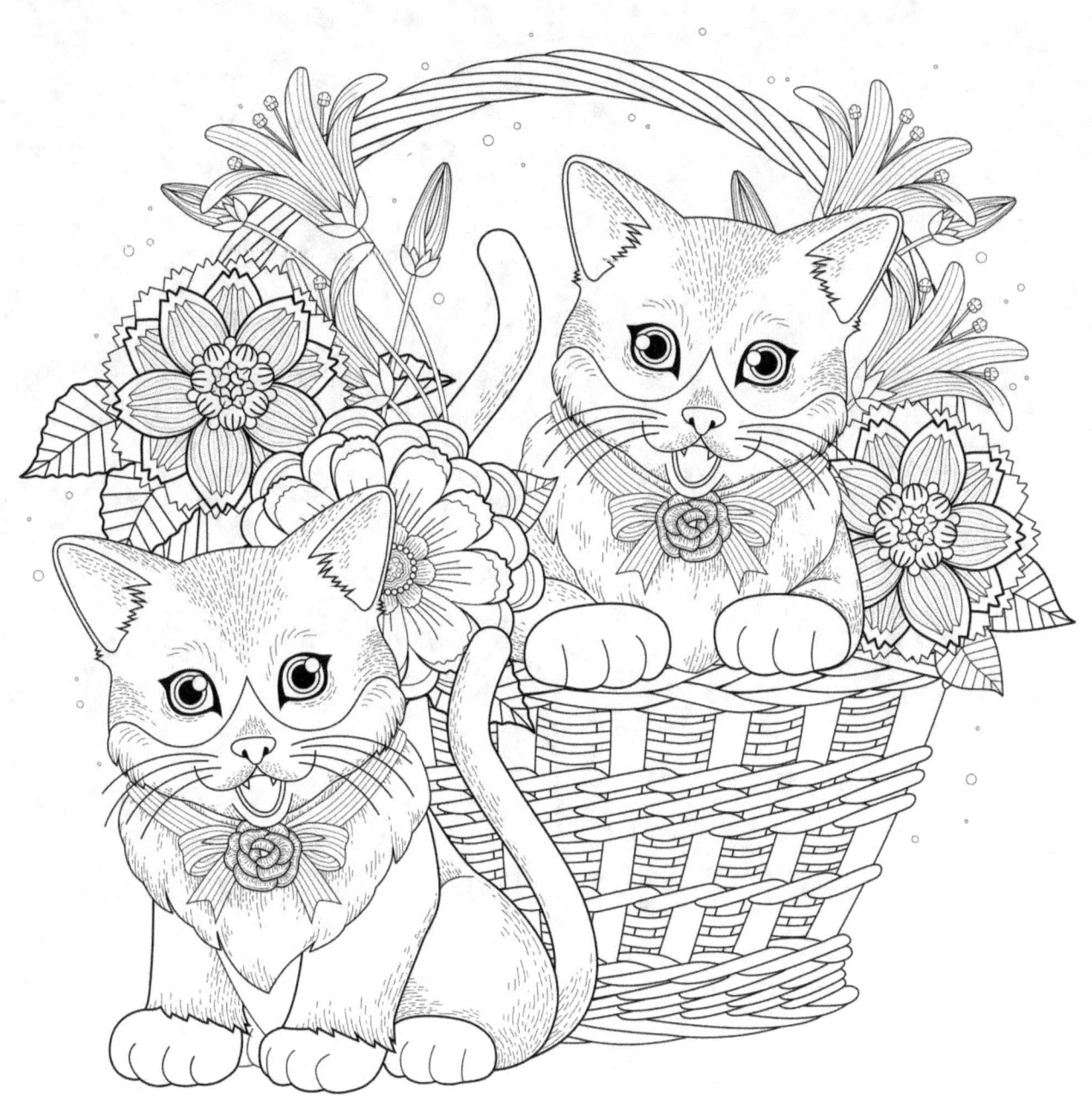

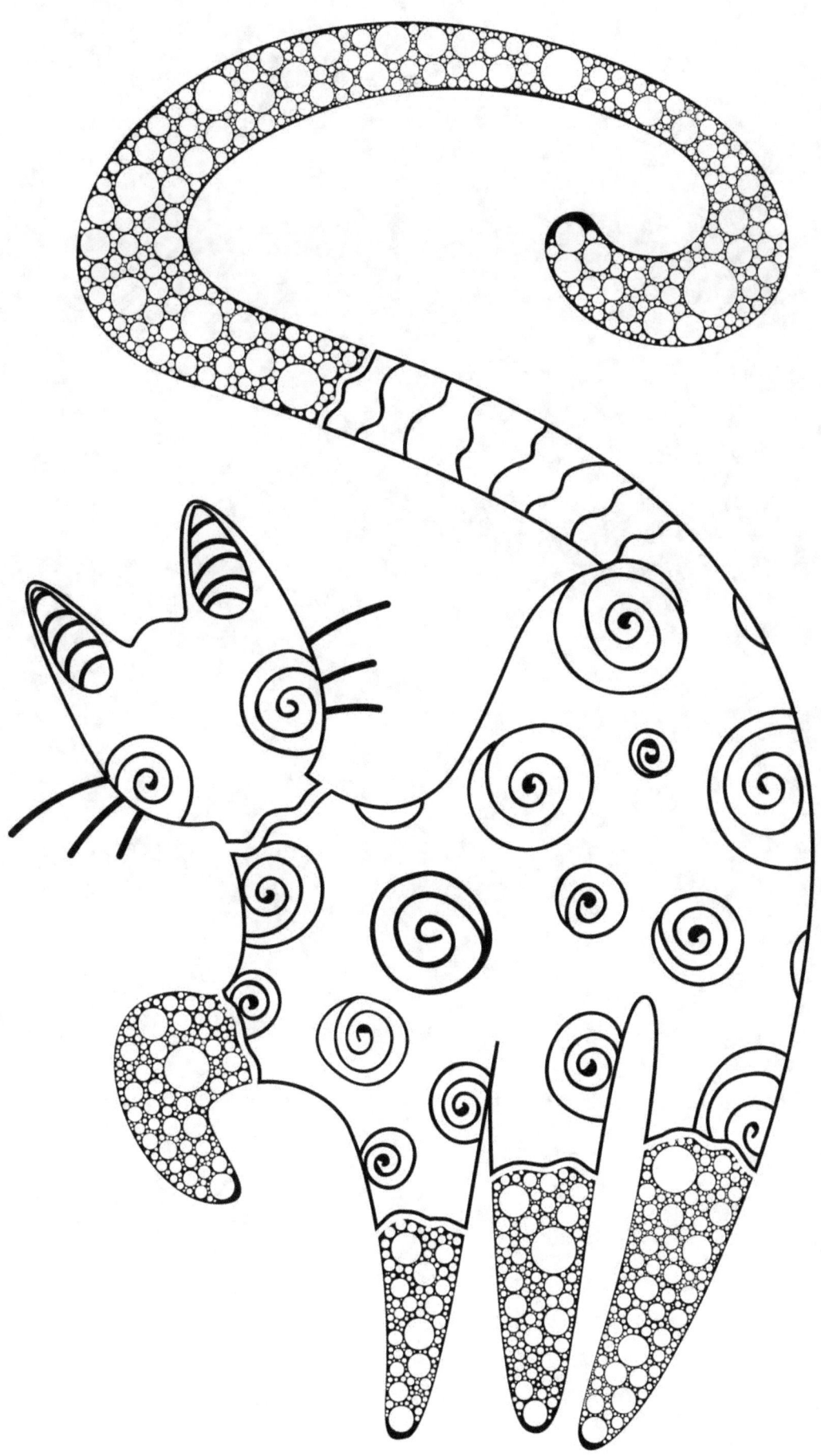

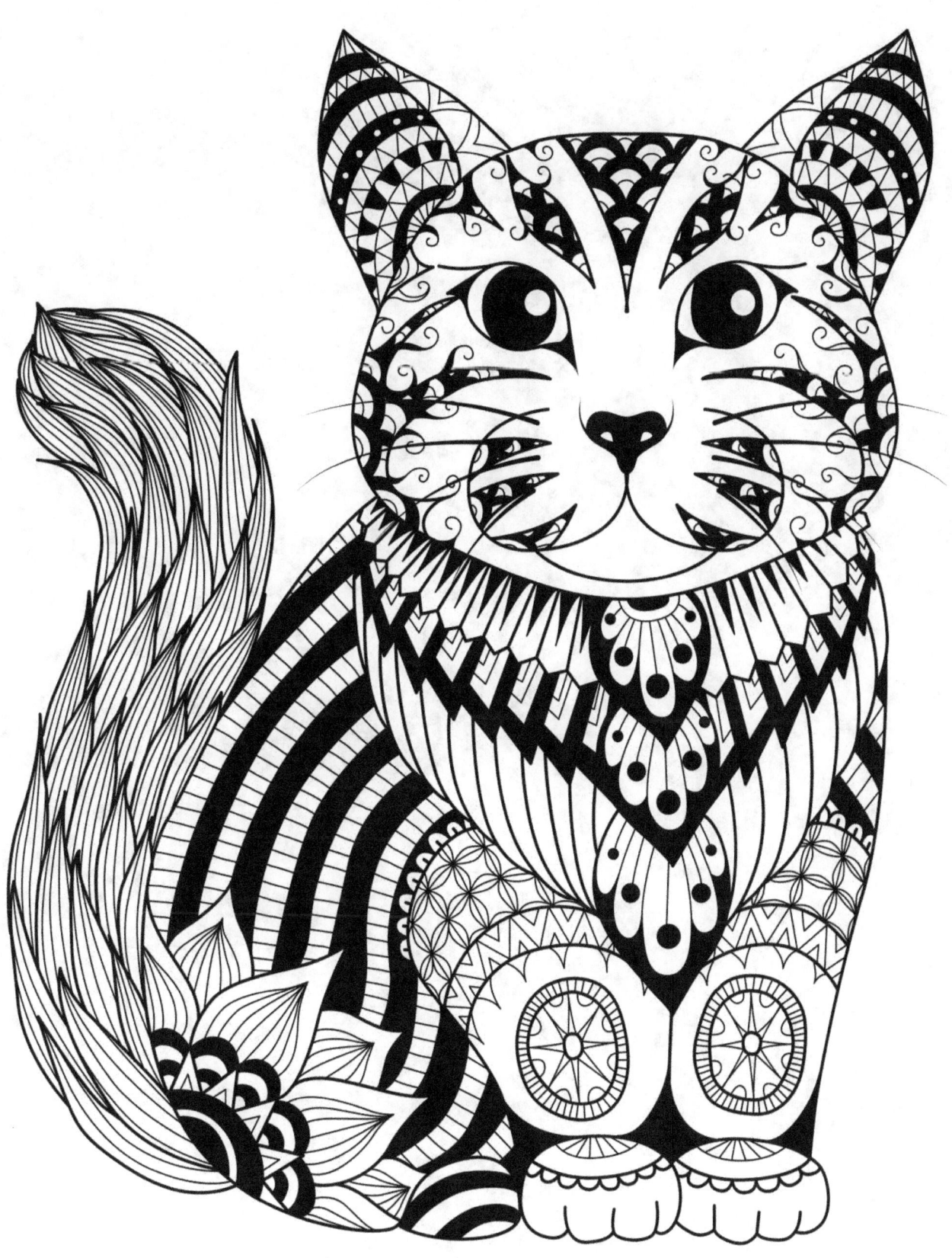

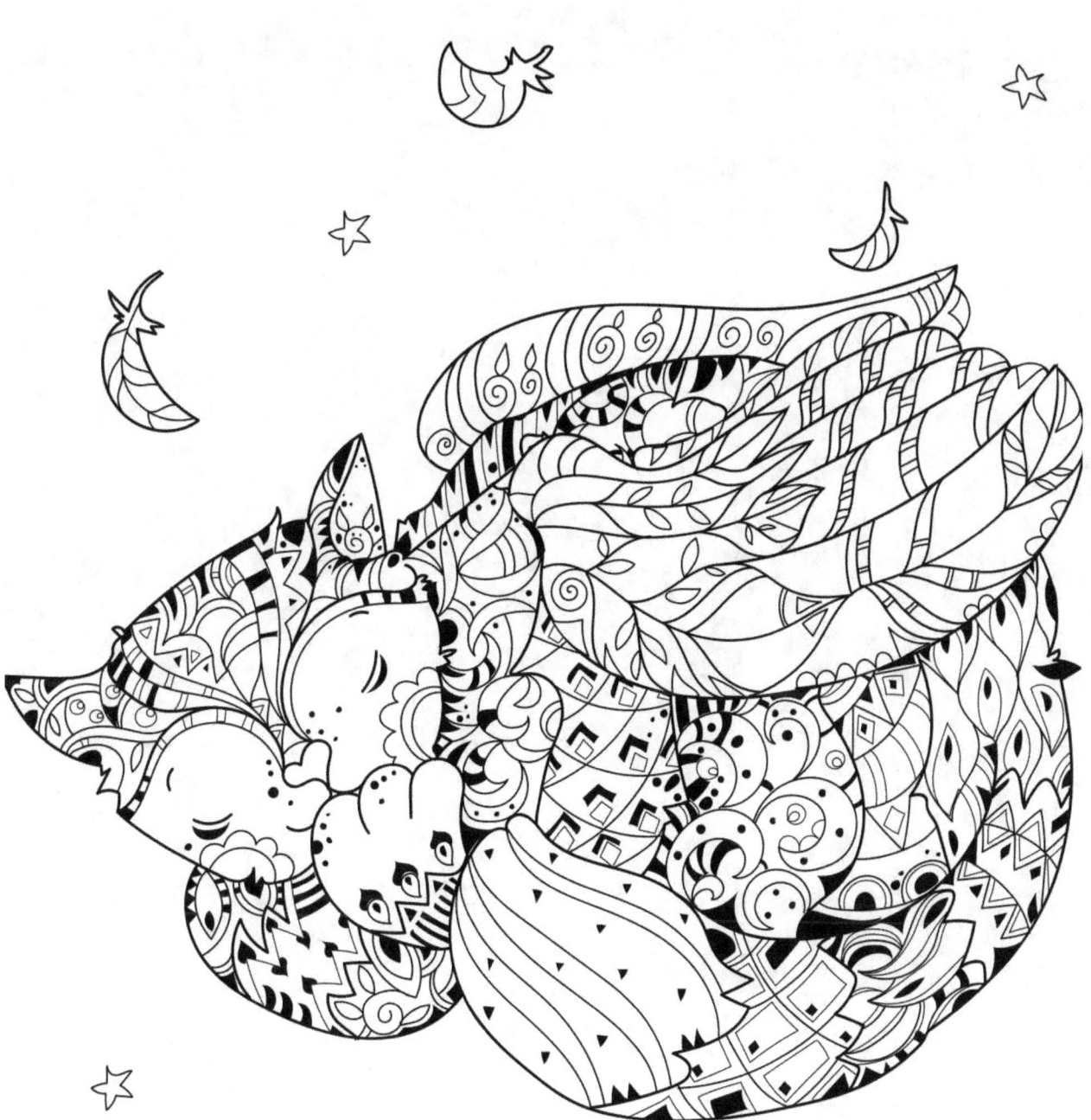

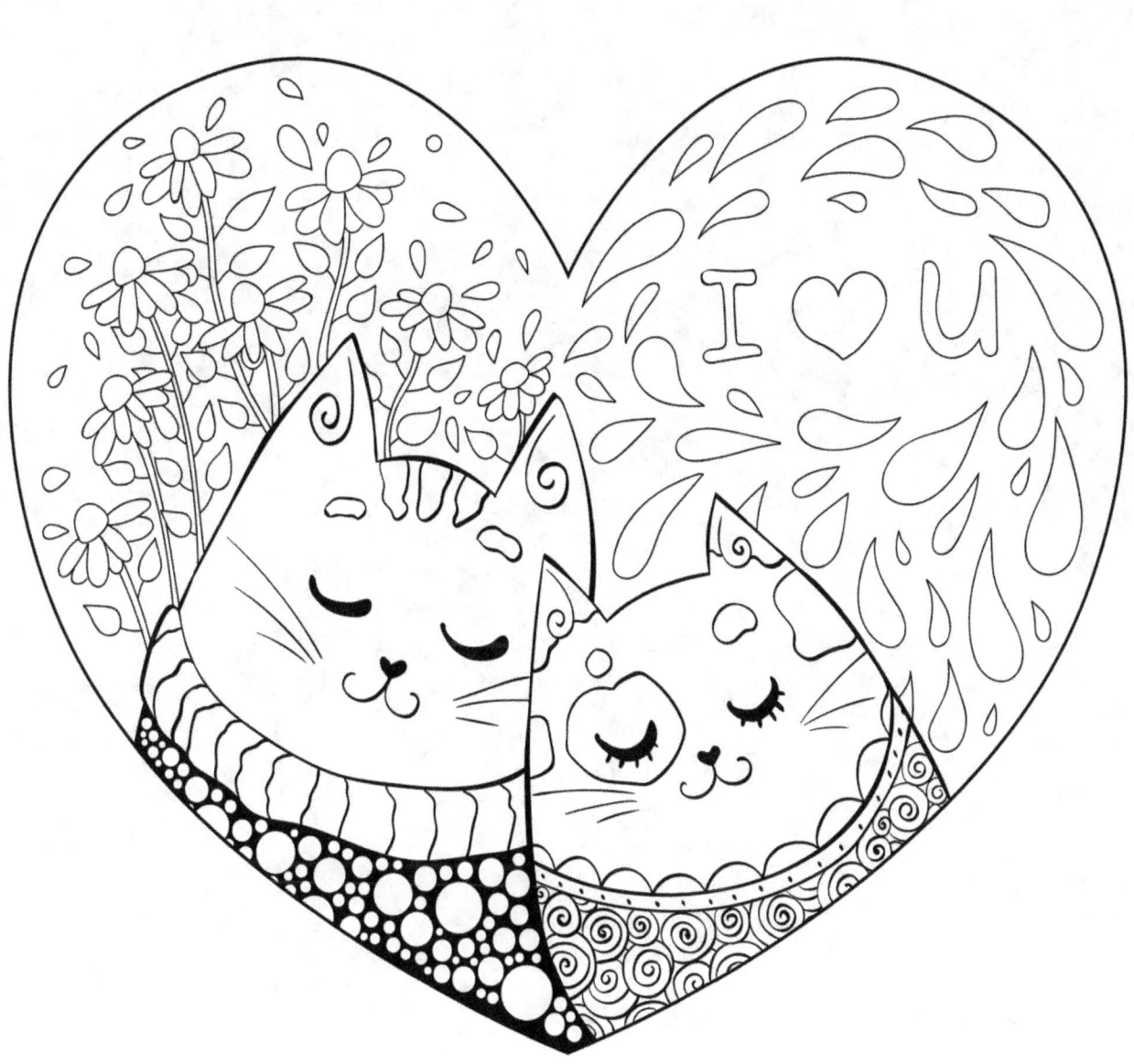

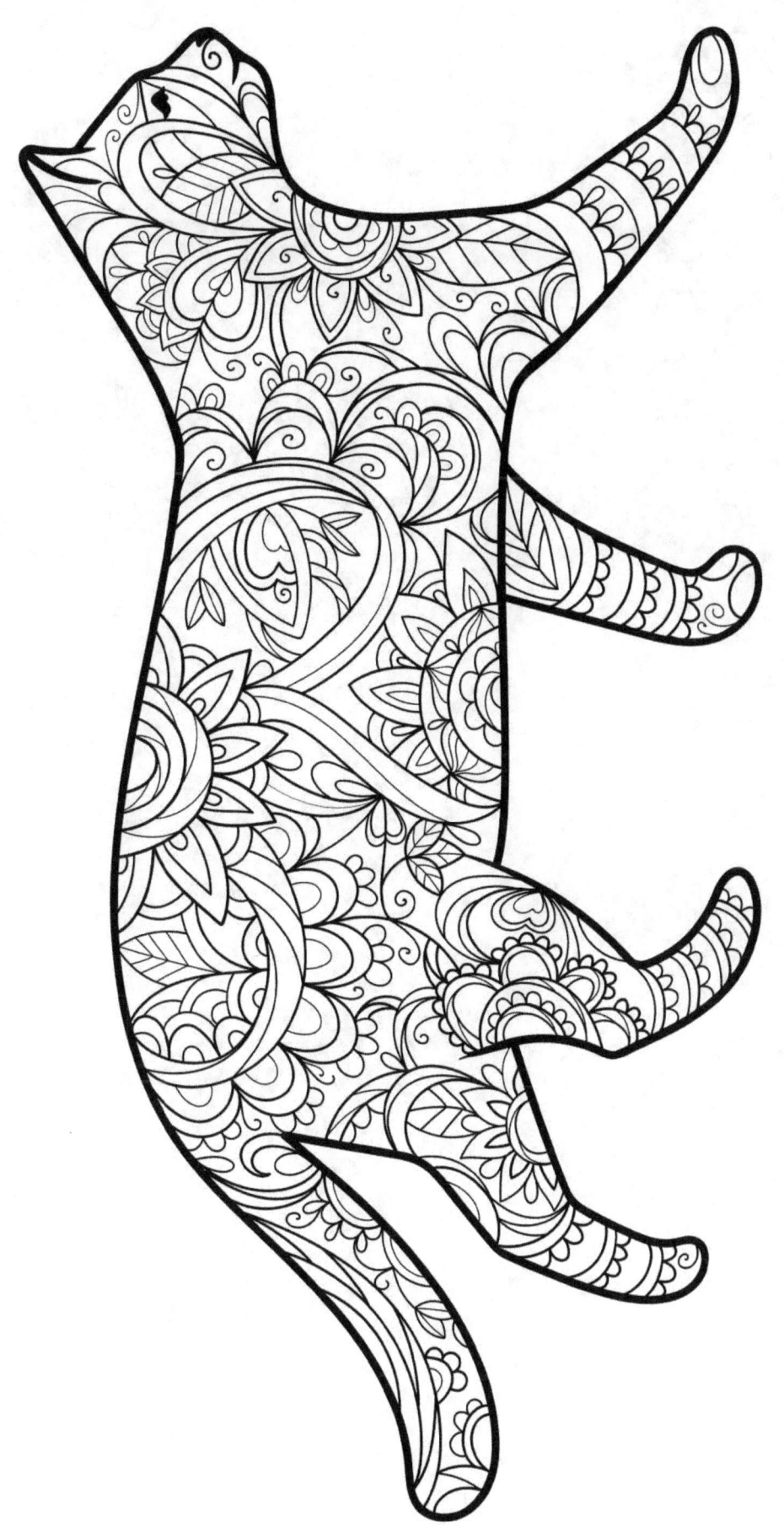

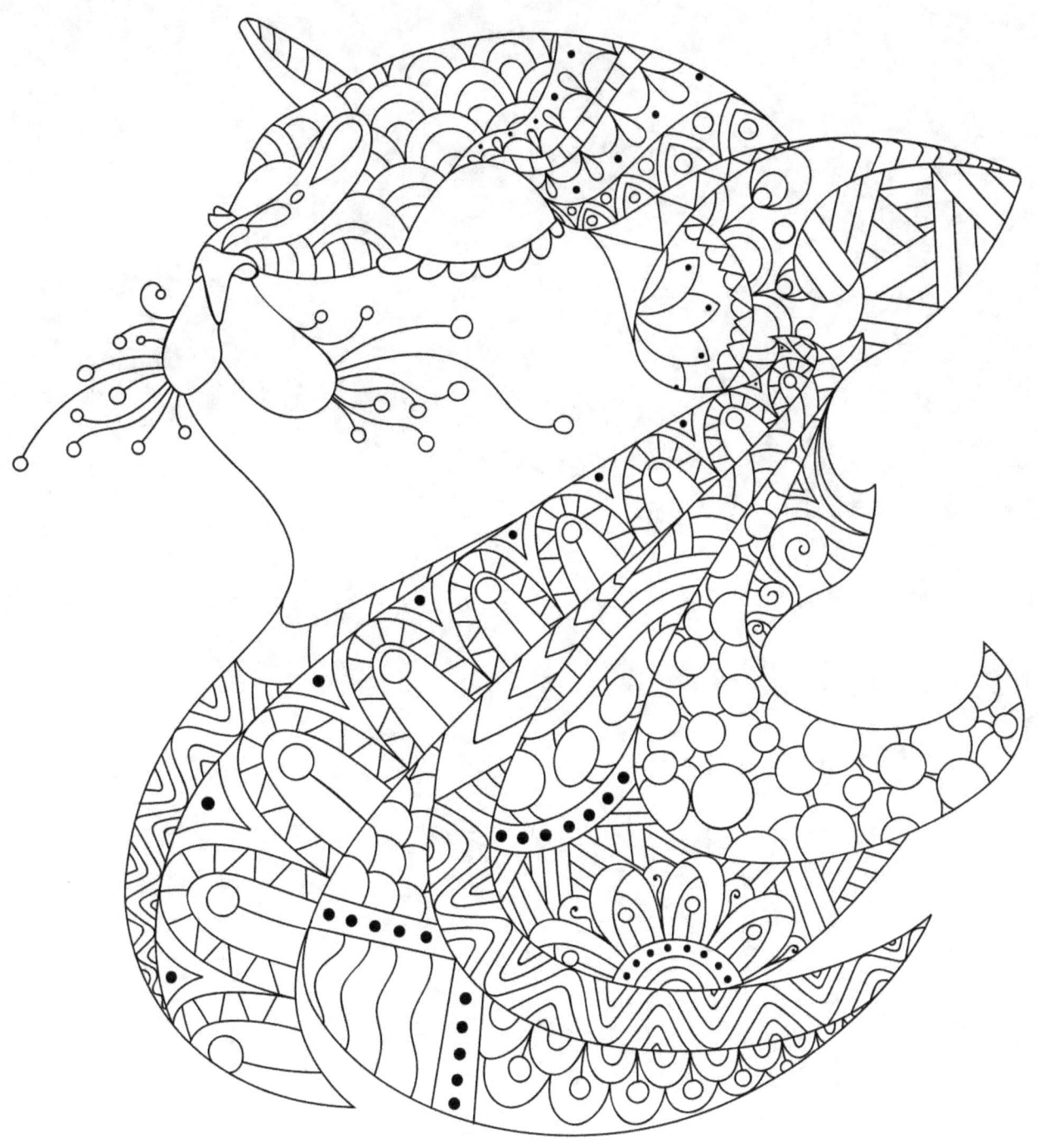

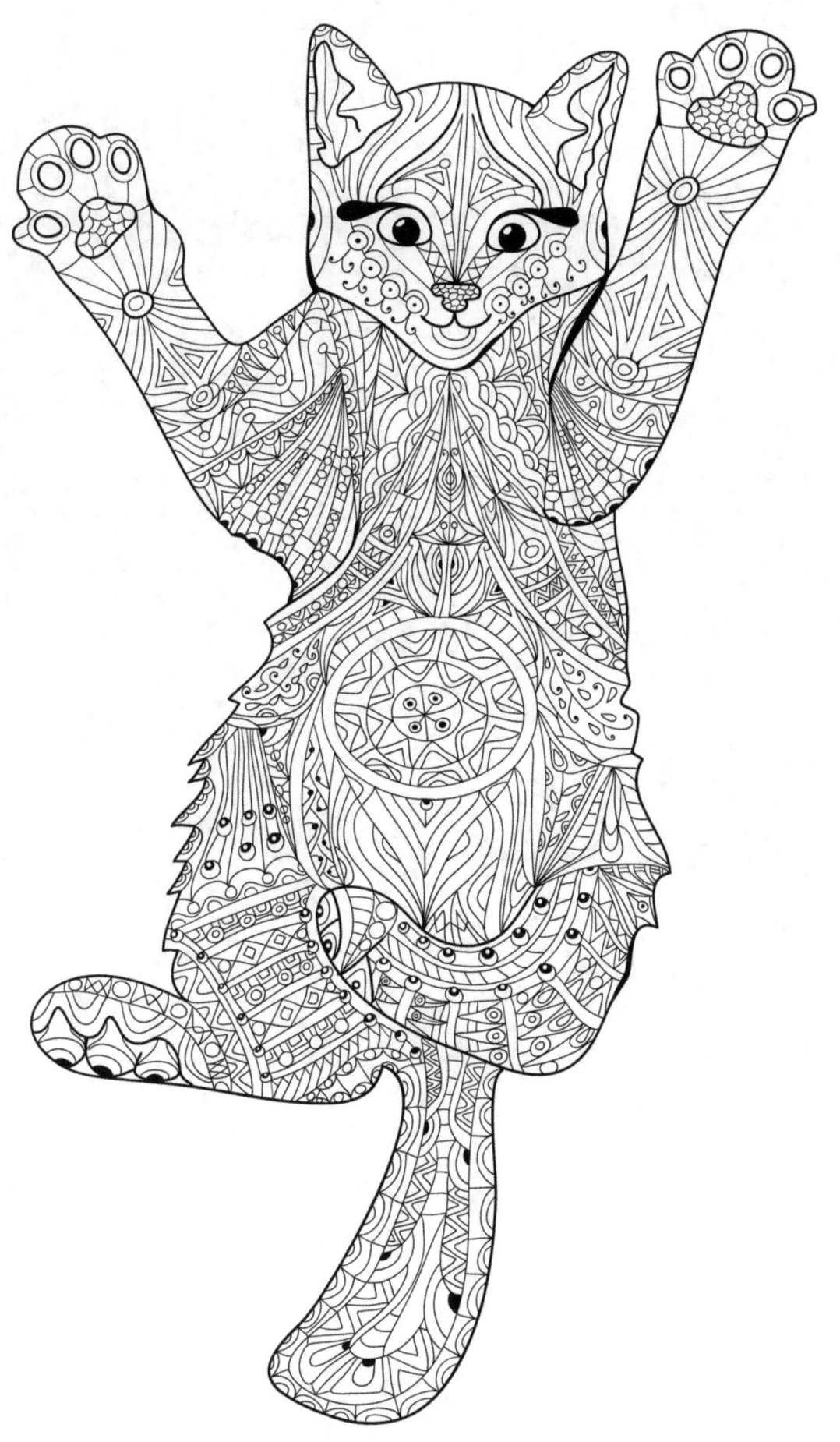

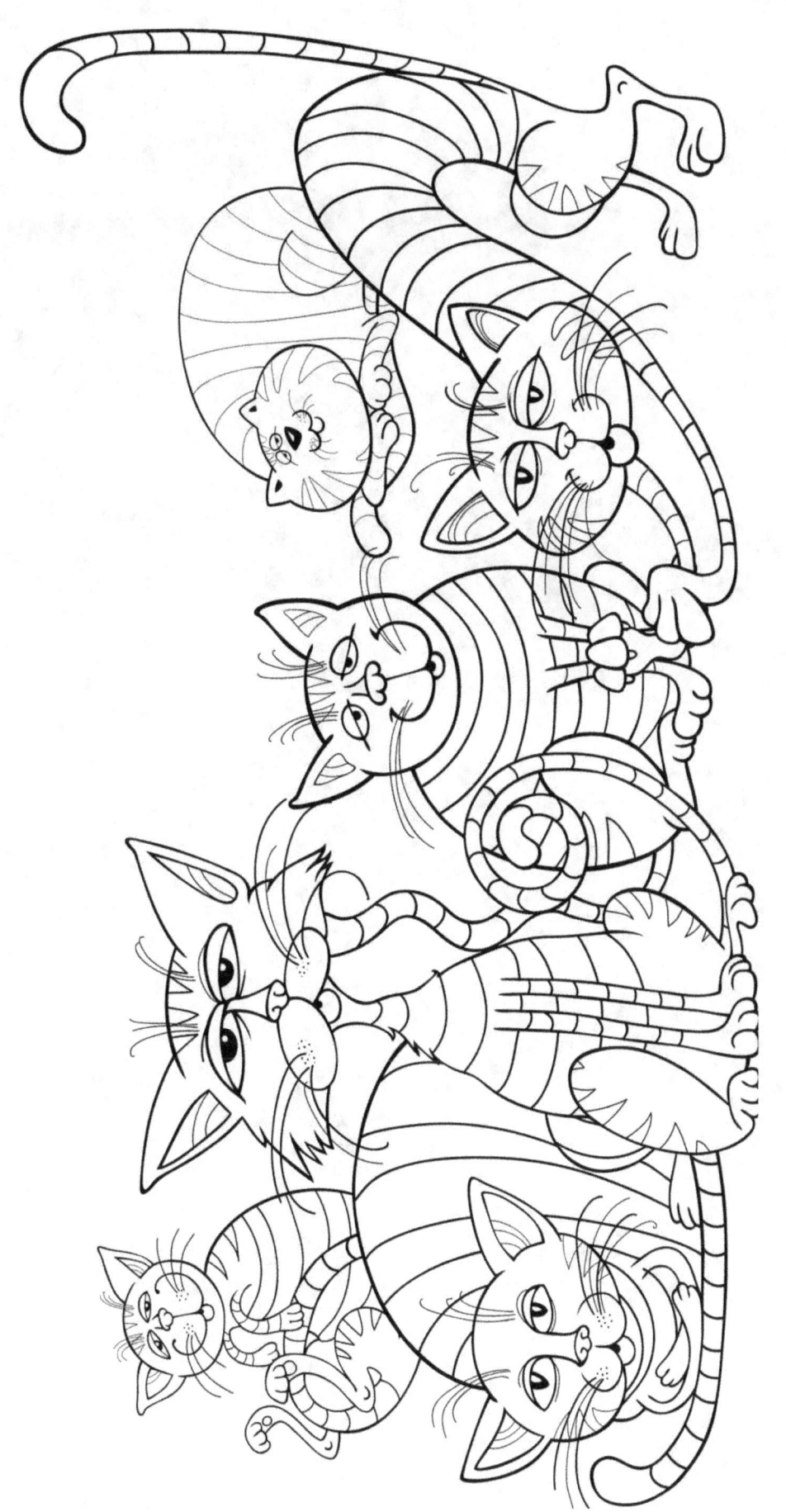

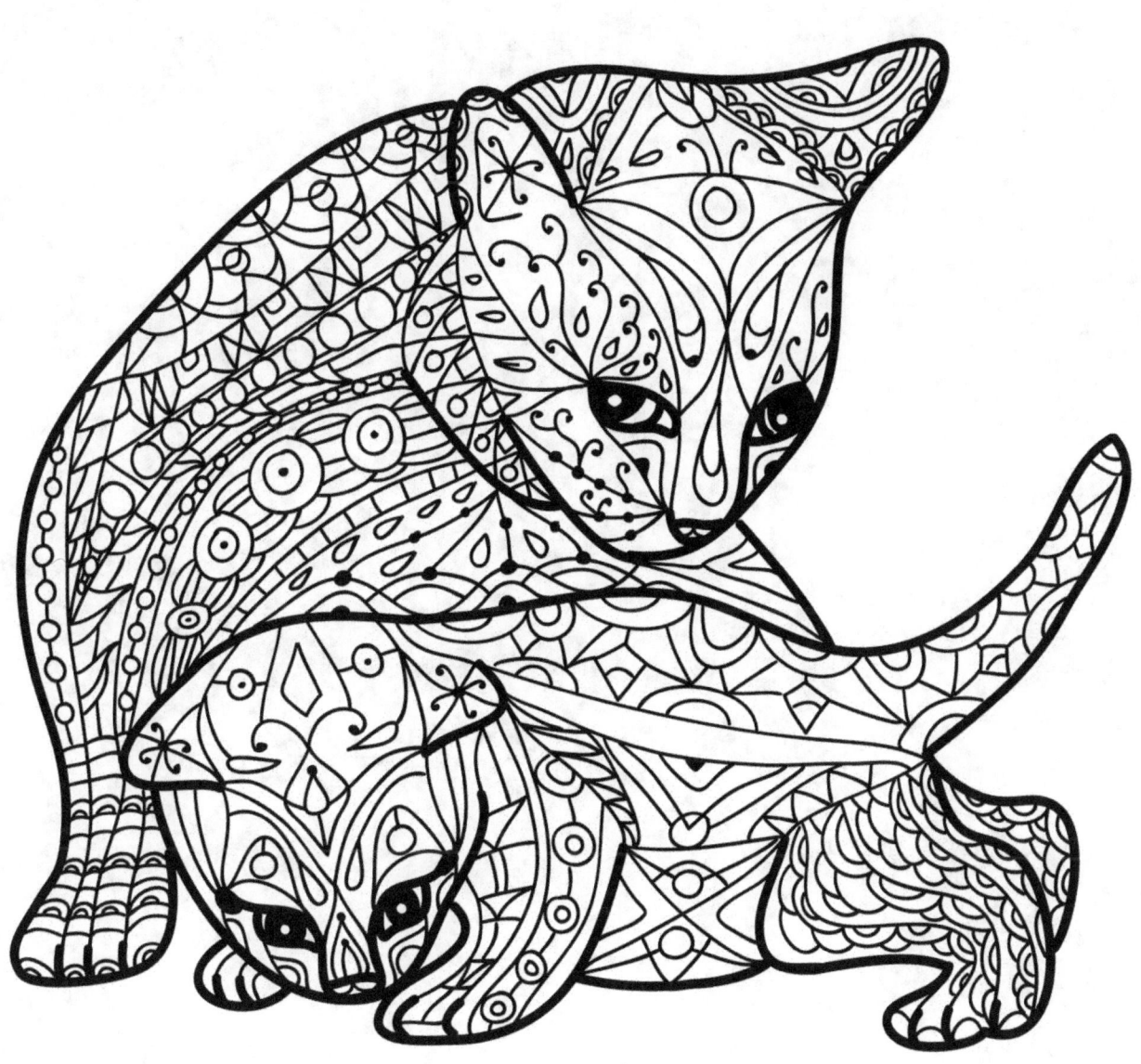

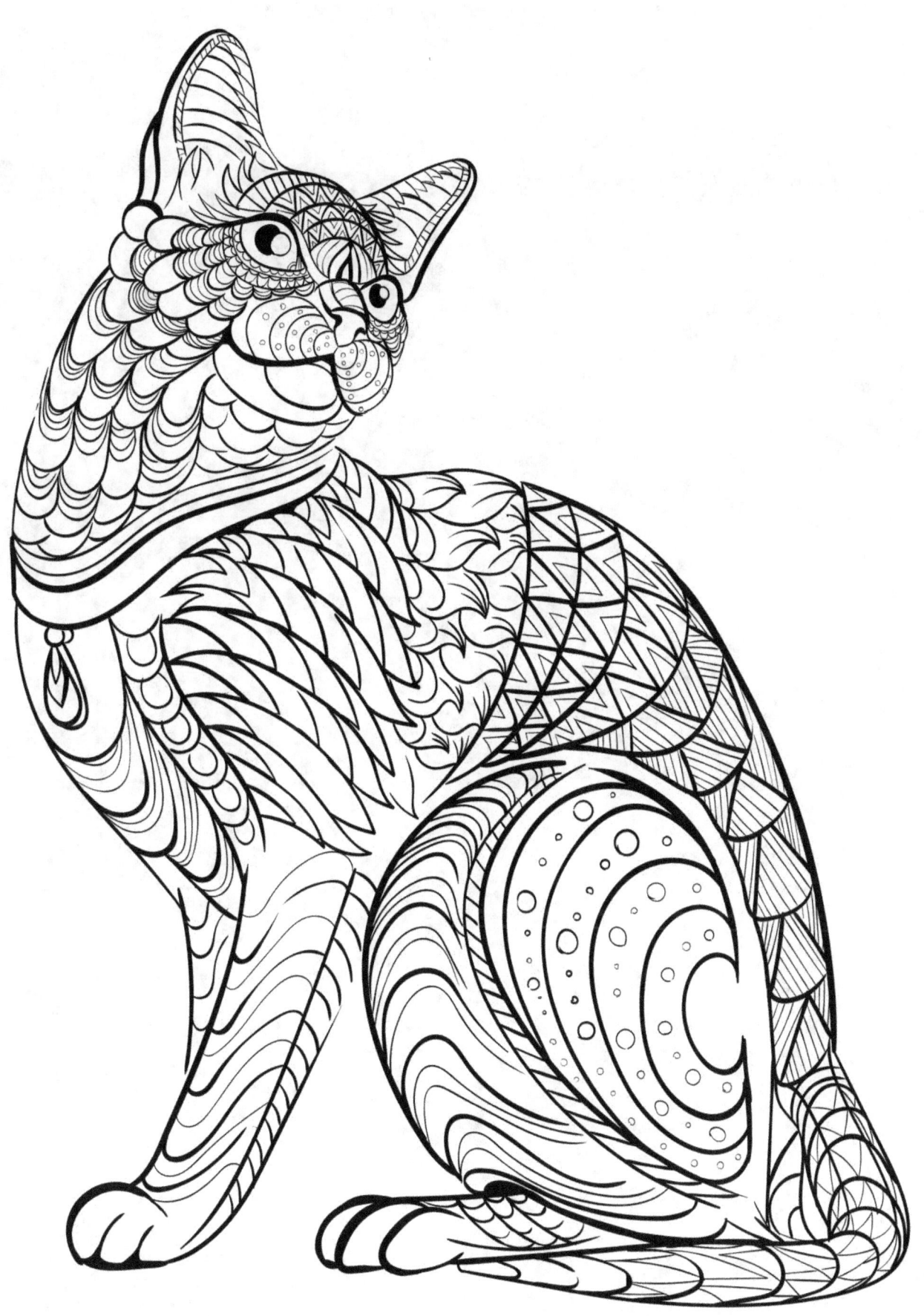

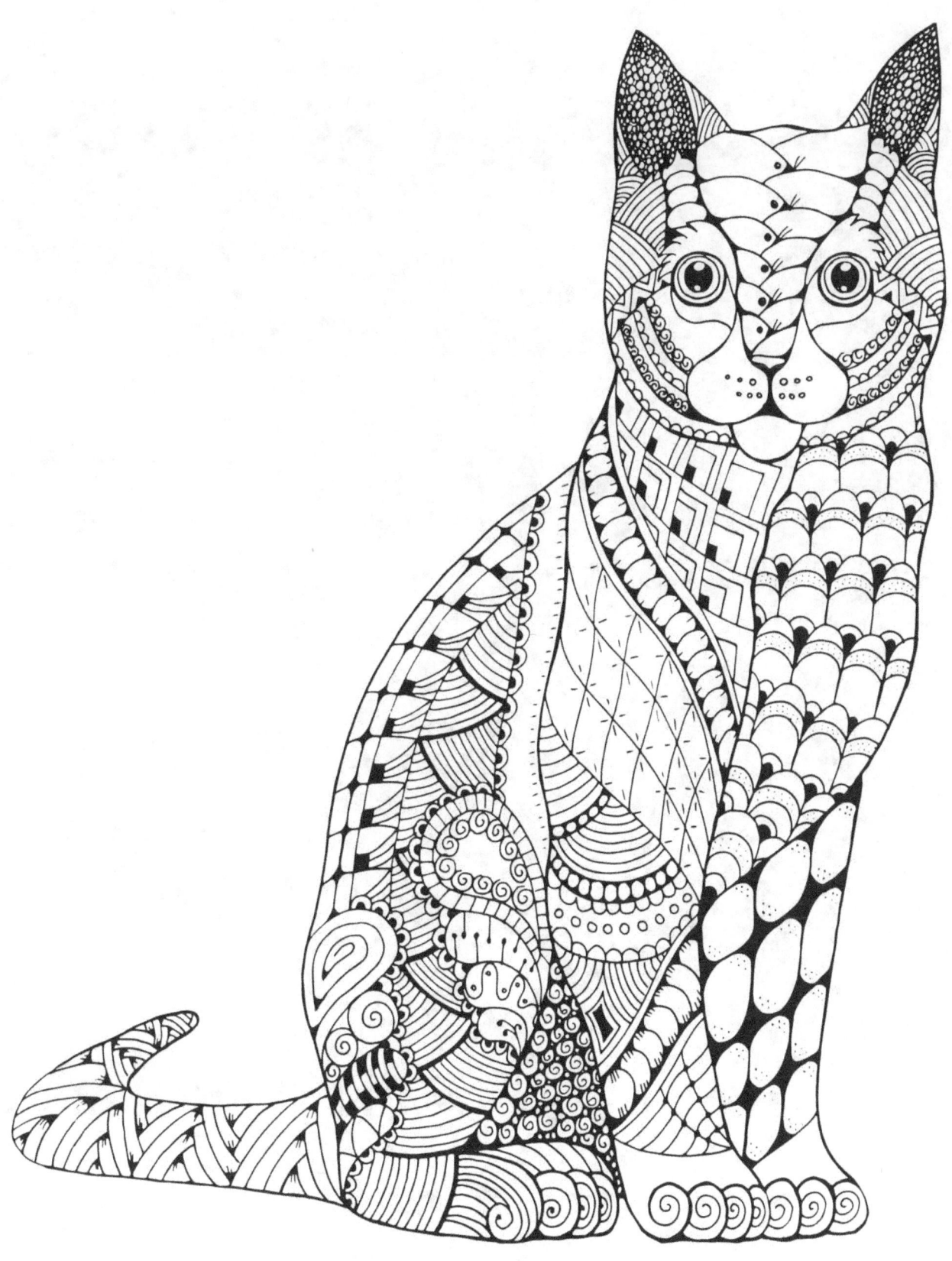

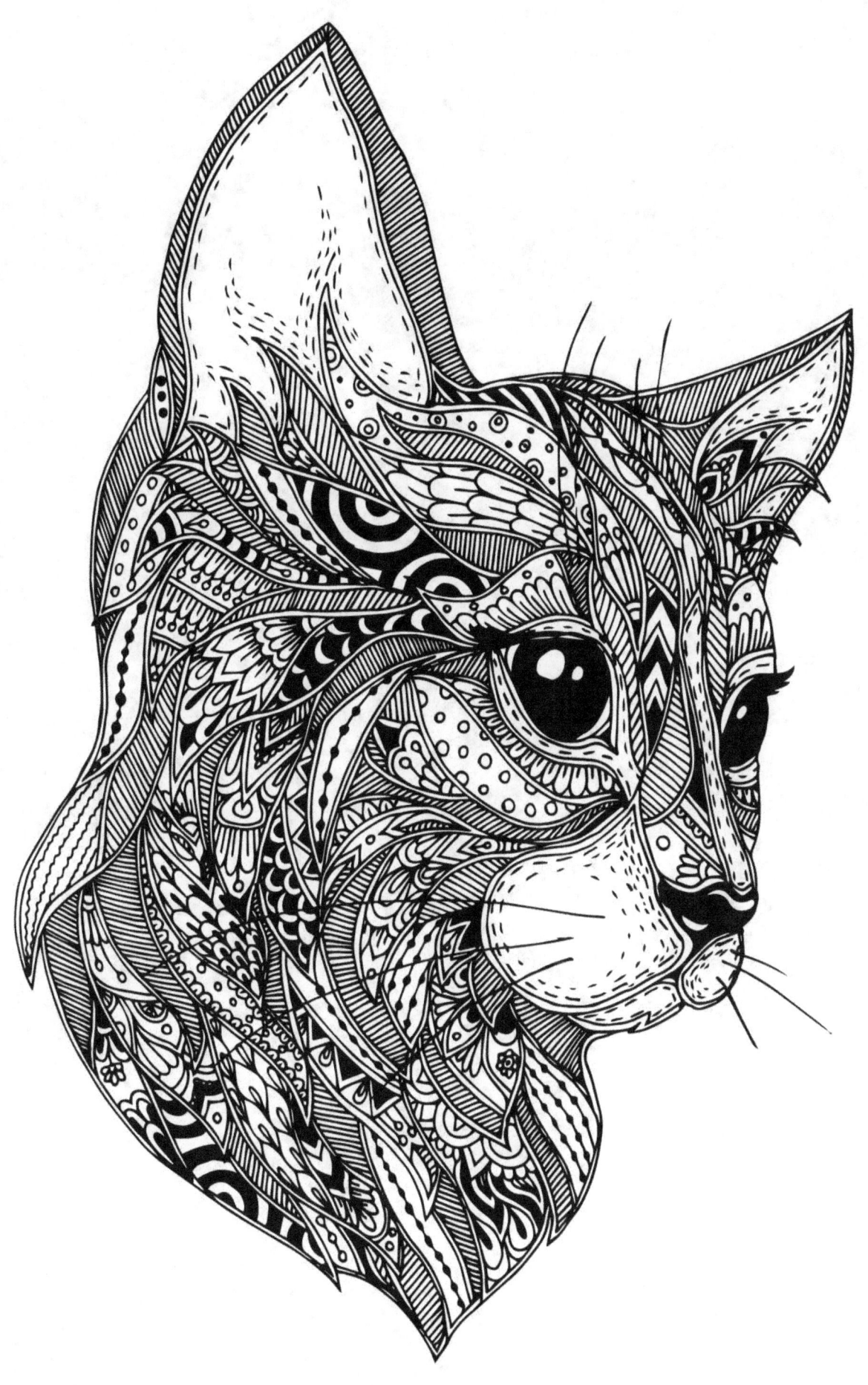

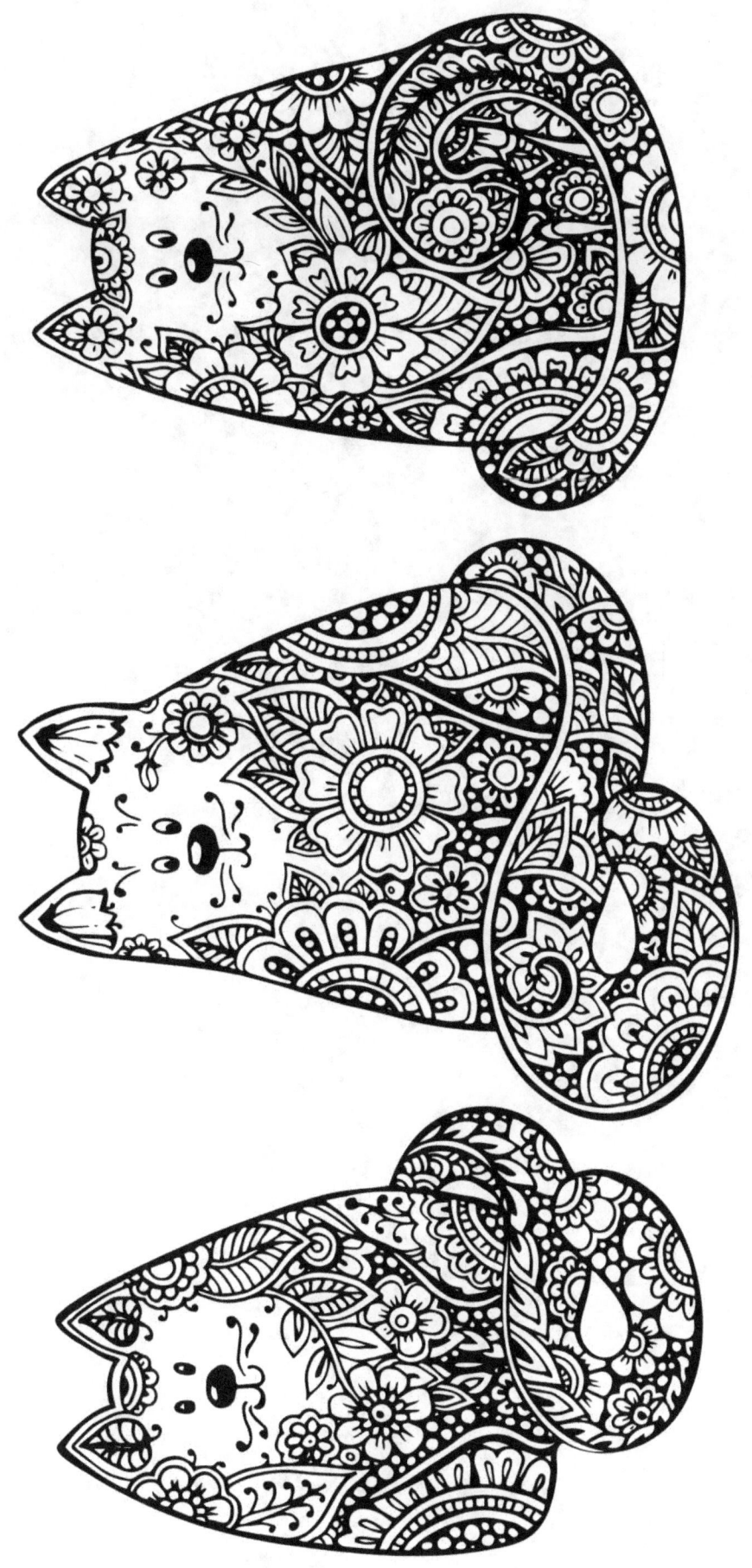

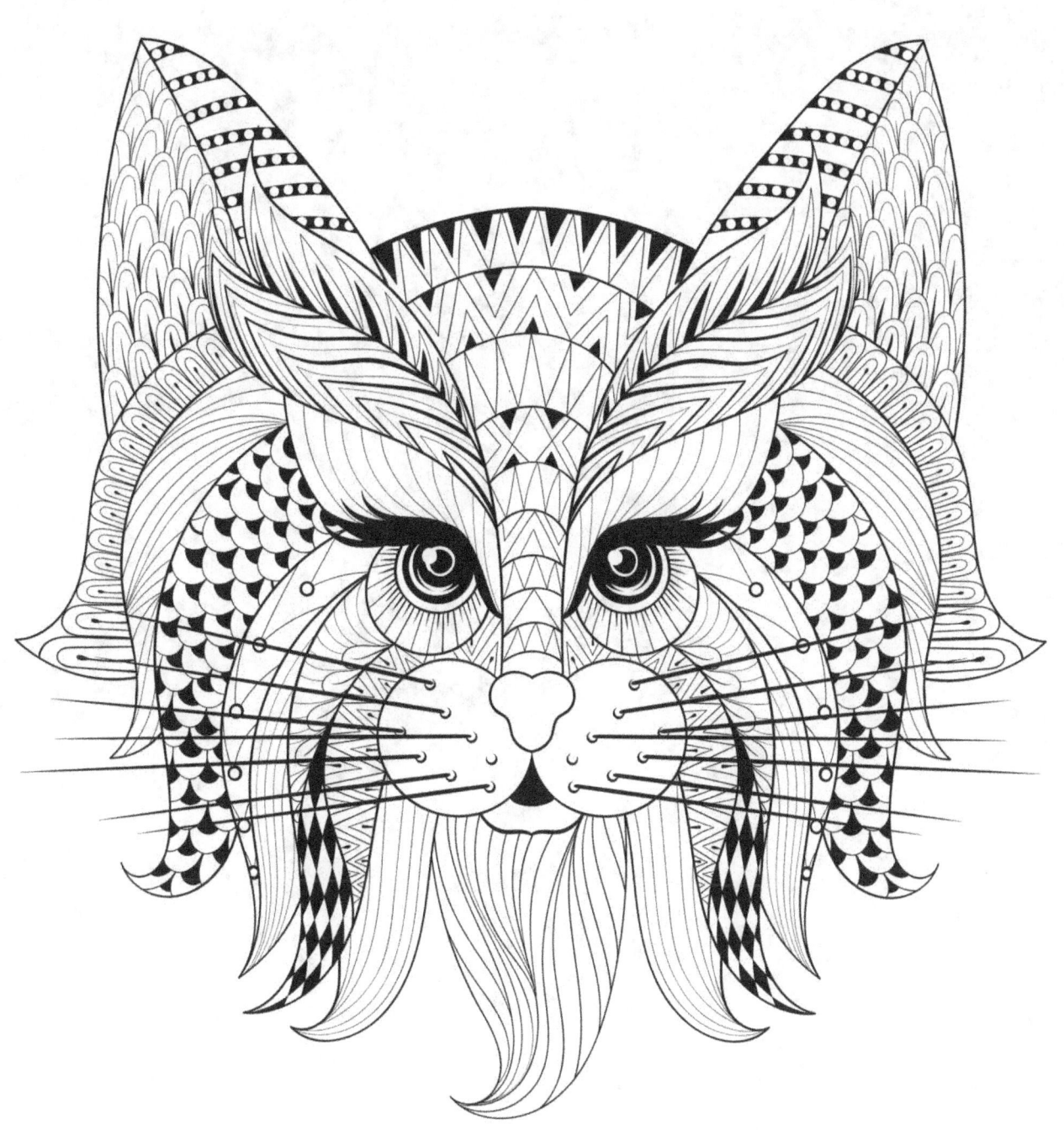

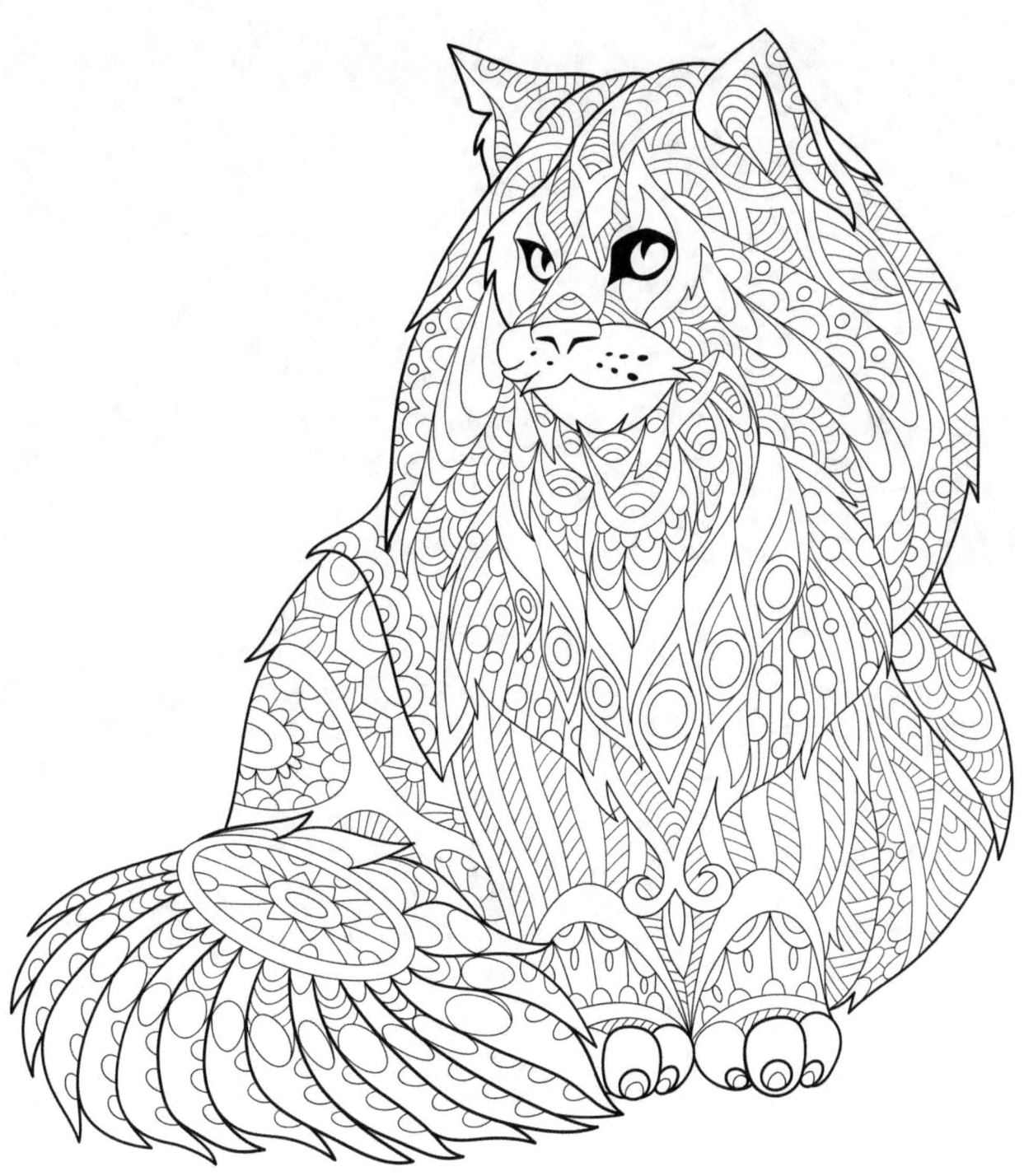

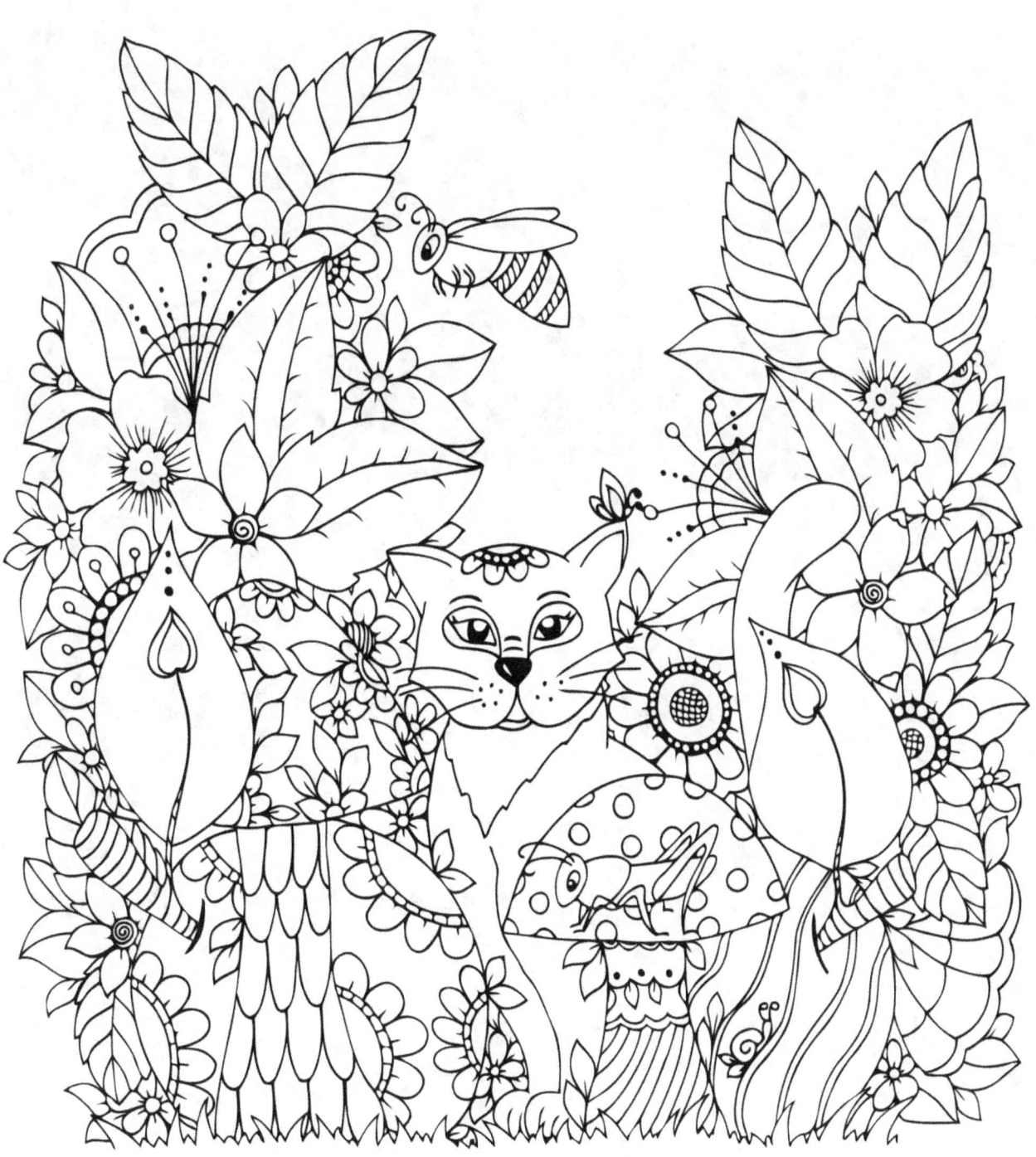

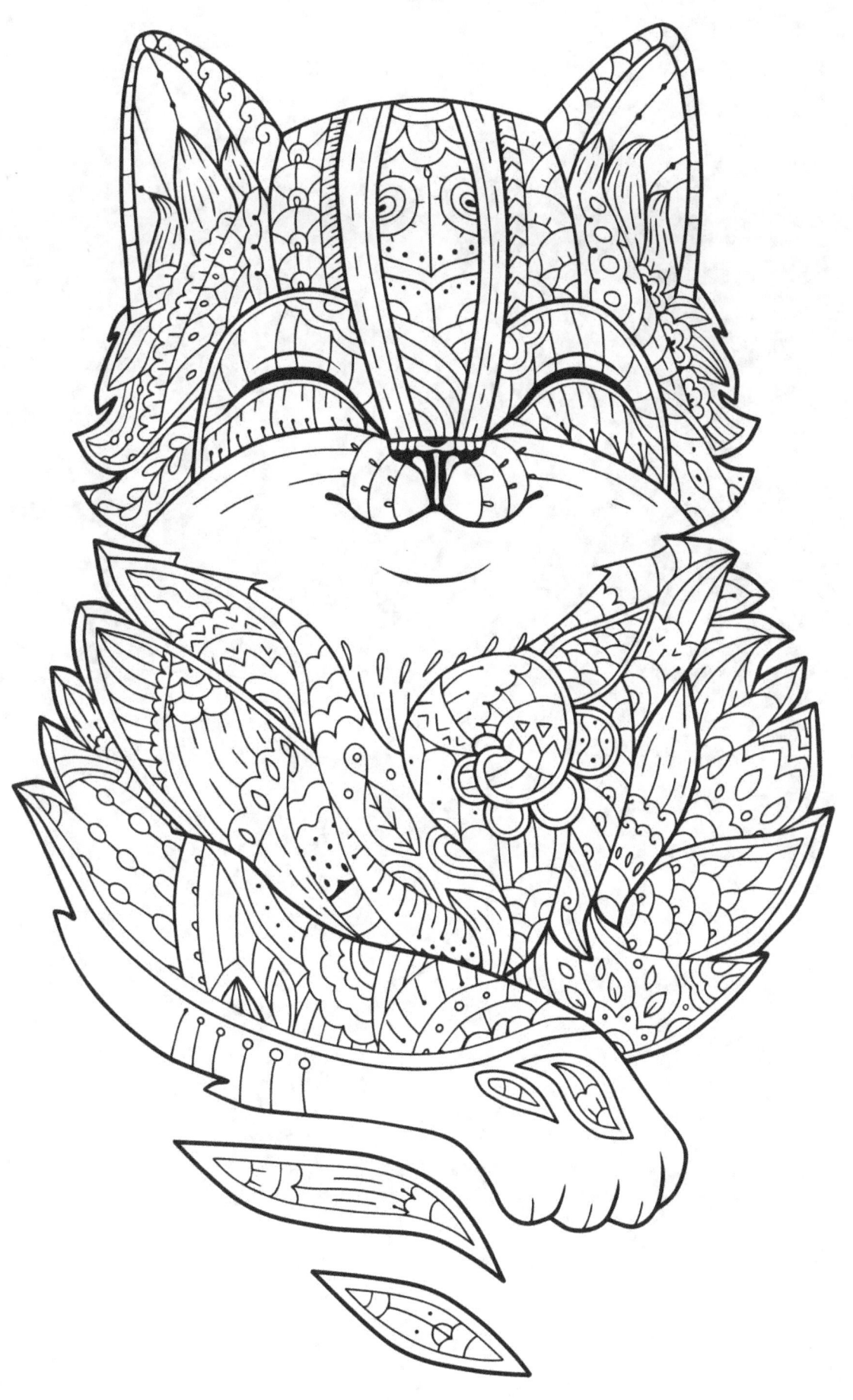

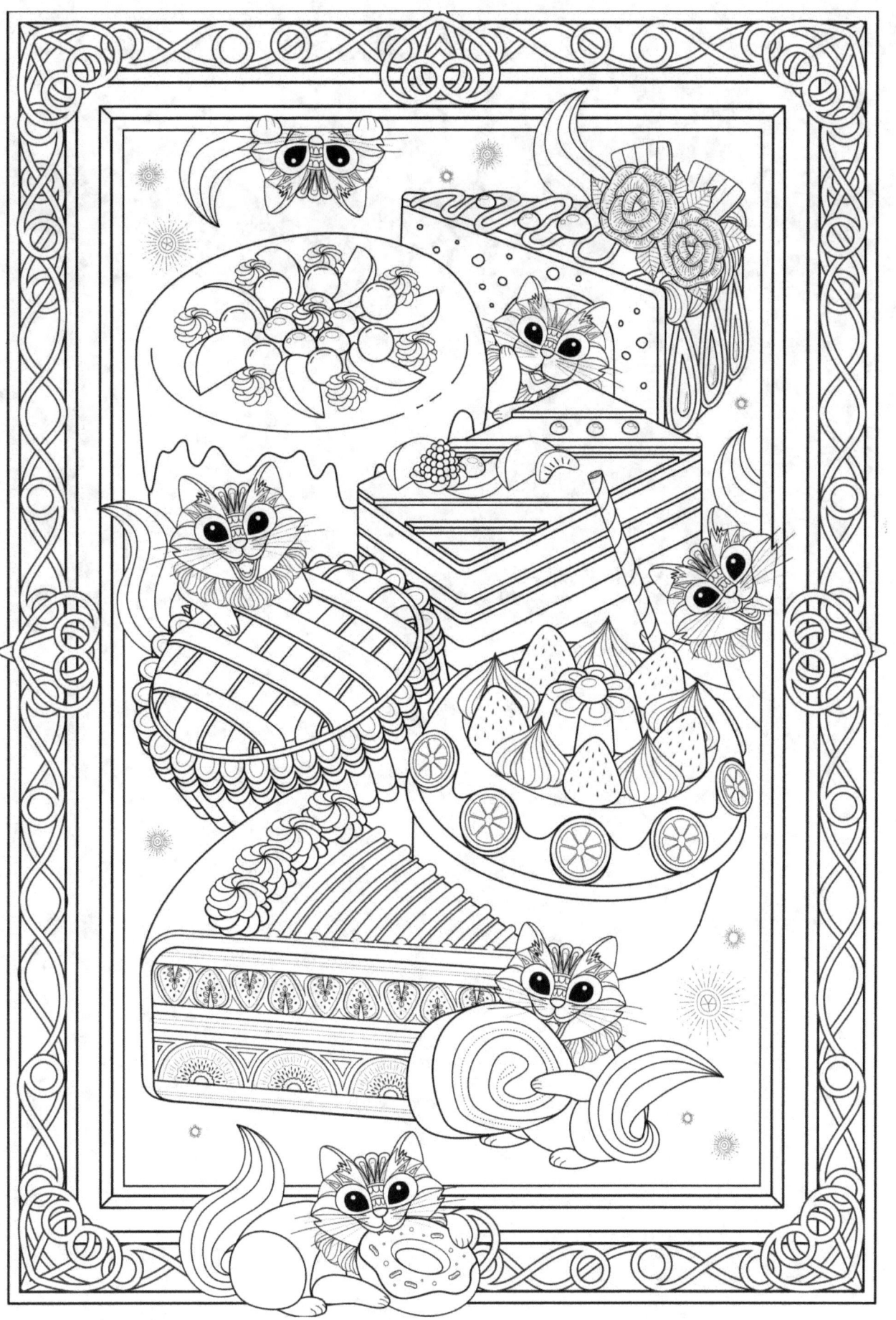

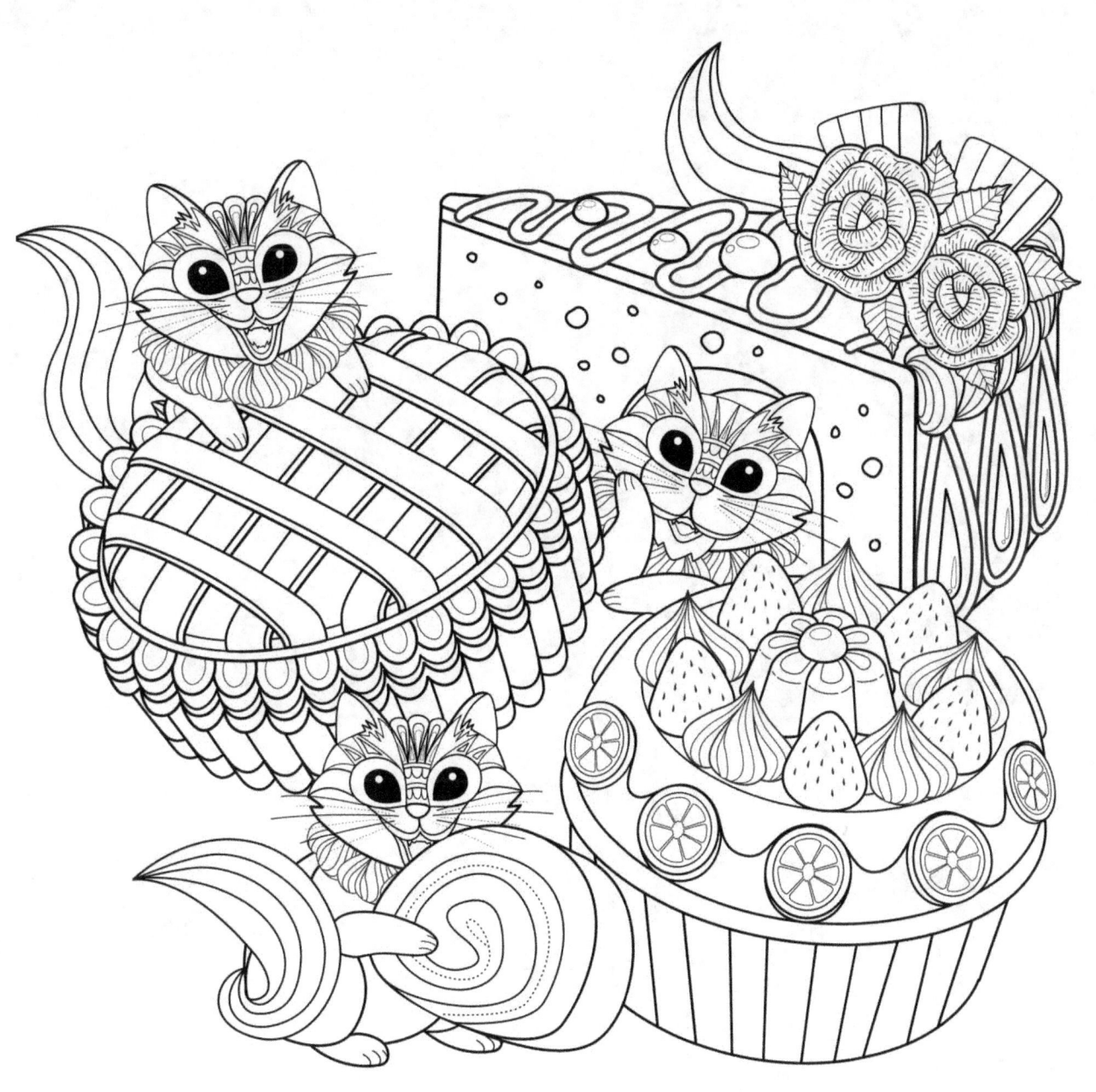

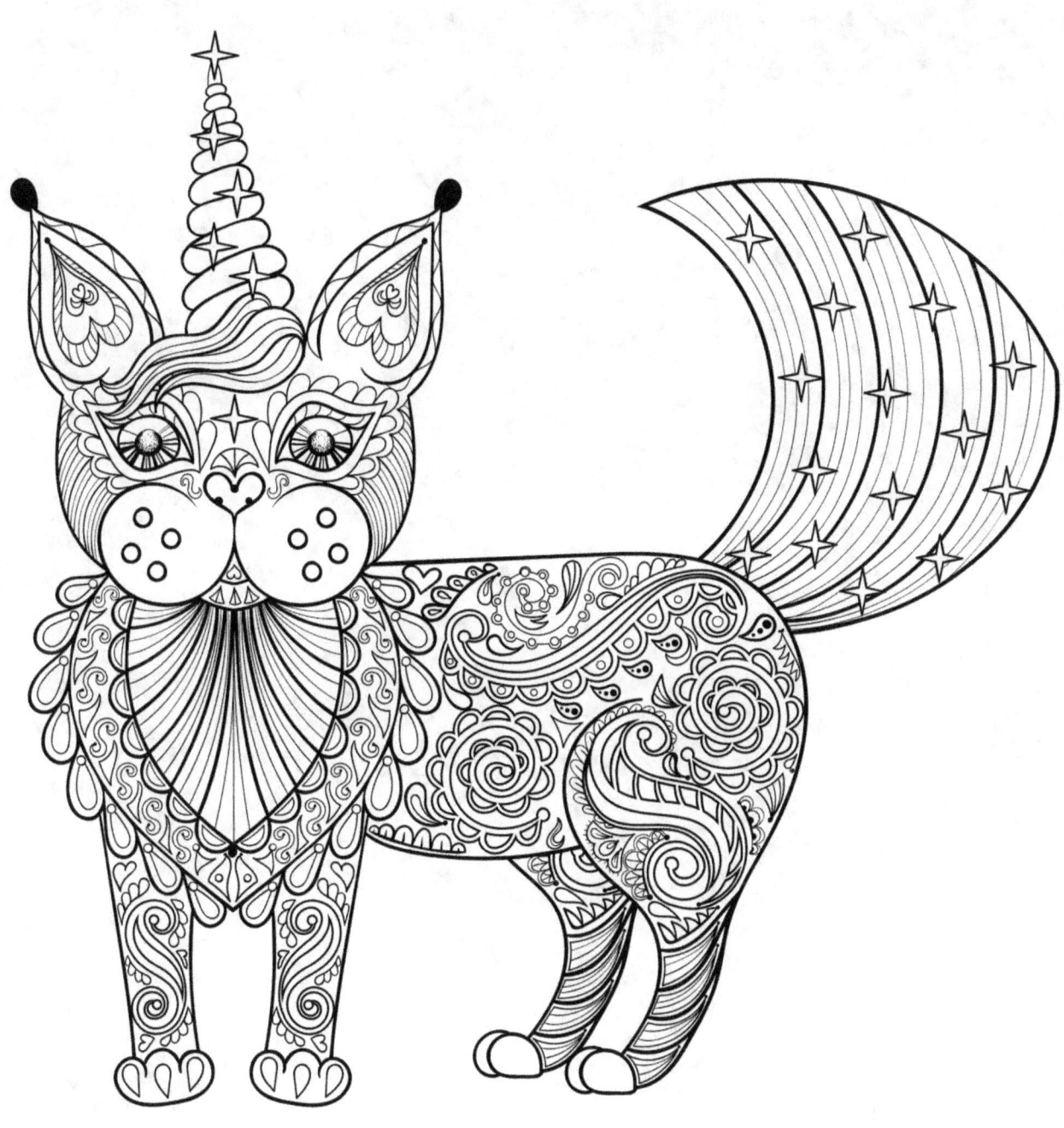

www.ingramcontent.com/pod-product-compliance
Lightning Source LLC
Chambersburg PA
CBHW081300180526
45170CB00007B/2503

* 9 781541 228085 *